Life Among The Wildflowers

Laura Beames

BookLeaf
Publishing

India | USA | UK

Presentation by *BookLeaf Publishing*

Web: www.bookleafpub.com

E-mail: info@bookleafpub.com

ISBN: 978-93-5744-937-3

First edition 2022

DEDICATION

To the boys who broke my heart, to the men yet
to appreciate it, and to the friends and family
who never cease to heal it.

ACKNOWLEDGEMENT

I have a lot of people to thank for this collection
of poetry, three friends in particular. Monique -
always willing and eager to read and critique my
poems, Ash - with her never ending wisdom,
and Kate - with her firm convictions. My
warriors - always willing to fight my battles
along side me.
Just as equally, to all of my family, friends, and
loved ones, for your endless support through
life.

PREFACE

On love, loss, and self-discovery.

Wildflower

He was never just another
So much worse than the rest
Her heart was neatly wrapped
Proudly mounted on a crest

A gift so freely given
A gift so undeserved
A gift she gave so willingly
Yet his always so reserved

He took her to the place
Her heart so full of trust
He took what she had given
He turned it into rust

Numbness blanketed her skin
Her heart feeling nothing at all
Little did she realise
So much good would come from this fall

She was never his to break
She was never meant to be owned
She fell because she had to
But that heart was only on loan

Unwittingly caged like a bird
By that supposed love
She had now been set free
With one last painful shove

Always treated as a ghost
A shadow so easily ignored
But he's the one that lost
His love nothing but flawed

What does love look like?
Pain and endless lies?
No, love is in her mirror
She sees it in her eyes

What is she without him
A shatter in the glass
She was much more after the break
A bird or flower in the grass

Now she roams the fields
Always wild, always free
It still surprises her to this day
A wildflower she was always meant to be

Face to the Sun

With beautiful petals
Surrounded by blades of grass
She may look delicate
But she is not made of glass

She'll sway gently in the wind
Her beauty will catch your eye
If you pull her from the stem
She'll learn how to fly

She's not just a flower
Beautiful, wild, and free
But with so much underneath
That most people can't see

She turns her face to the sun
Even as she turns her back on you
Desperate to bask in the warmth
Desperate to dance freely too

Forever roaming the fields
Living the fullest of lives
She'll soak up all that is good
And just like that, always thrives

Girl in a Box

Wind her up
Watch her dance
Open that lid
Give her a chance

She'll dance for you
Like she has a choice
But while she dances
She has no voice

Around in circles
The music plays
Over and over
It will play for days

When he's done
He'll shut the top
Her dancing may cease
But her heart won't stop

Gilded Cage

Swirls of gold
Bars of steel
The gilded cage
Was all too real

Beautiful and hard
Cold to the touch
She was meant to be free
But that never meant much

He shuts the door
He turns the key
Suddenly she's trapped
Like a bird from a tree

She'll stretch those wings
They don't get far
They're met with resistance
In the form of a steel bar

She can taste the freedom
See it through the cage
It's all so close
But feels further with age

She tries again
To stretch those wings
She let's her soul loose
This bird starts to sing

Breaking through steel
Is painfully tough
But it was always in her
To fly through the rough

Dear Mum & Dad

Dear mum and dad
Will you hold my hand?
I know I'm older now
But I still need help to land

I've stretched out my wings
I'm learning to fly
But I'll always need you
No matter how hard I try

I've been oh so stubborn
I never truly understood
That your love for me is endless
That you did everything you could

Like a small ball of light
Sitting in my chest
I can feel all that love
So much larger than the rest

I can see it now
I can't thank you enough
All that endless support
Through everything so tough

My heart I gift you
Wrapped in a bow with a curl
Dear mum and dad
Always, your little girl

Rebellious Heart

It pulses my veins
It's under my skin
The need to breathe
Like a beautiful sin

I crave the freedom
To be wholly mine
Not share myself
Nor share my time

It isn't yours
It can't be owned
This heart is free
It can only be loaned

My starved lungs crave
The sweet fresh air
It burns my throat
But I don't care

My life is my own
Not yours to claim
You may be my partner
But I'm not yours to tame

My blood pumps the poison
Through my rebellious heart
It catches on an ember
While fire tears it apart

Shooting Star

She soars
Like a bright shooting star
And explodes
Into everything that you are

Awaken

It's in the sky
It's in the waves
What the weather starts
Her soul will crave

She feels the water
Around her waist
With a gentle pull
Salt she can taste

It becomes tumultuous
Like her beating heart
That gentle pull
Was never gentle to start

She starts to swim
She tries too much
To reach that point
To the sand she'll clutch

It falls away
Beneath her feet
Pulling her further
She never could cheat

Desperation claws
Right through her core
Like bloody arrows
Cutting her raw

Beneath the surface
Her breath is taken
As she drowns
Her soul will awaken

Disappear

I'm about to disappear
To jump on a plane
Never look back
And never be the same

You might say I'm running
You might say I'm scared
But what others think
I never truly cared

I'm chasing my happiness
I'm finding my way
And if you don't like that
That's pretty darn okay

The wheels leave the tarmac
The wind lifts the wings
As that plane takes off
My whole body, it sings

My heart feels release
Like it's never known
I have no regrets now
I'm finally home

Maybe She'll Stay

She can't be owned
She never could
She feels the confines
Of the box made of wood

Such a good man
A heart with all care
But can a free bird
Give its heart to share?

She pushes and thrashes
Fights what could be
She rebels against his love
To stay wild and free.

Maybe she'll run
Or maybe she'll stay
But she will stay free
In either which way

Always Mine

Each grain of sand
Holds a secret for me
This is my place to feel
To finally be free

No expectations
As the waves break the shore
I'm simply there for me
I couldn't ask for more

My feet feel the cold
As the water rushes in
It wakes up my soul
Like an exquisite sin

I raise my head to the sky
Feel the breeze brush my face
Closing my eyes
Freedom I taste

Stuck in this moment
This perfect piece in time
You may think you took it all
But this will always be mine

Thrill of the Fall

Nothing but wind beneath you
Nothing but fire in your veins
A rush that overtakes you
That refuses to be tamed

As you fall
You'll lose all sense
The thrill of the unknown
Is all too intense

You'll try to stop
But there's nothing to hold
That air that tickles your skin
Feeling suddenly so cold

That fear fills your lungs
Like ice cold water
You were once a person
You were once a daughter

You lose yourself
In the dread like a flame
Only to awaken
A new woman they can't claim

Siblings

When we were babies
We shared a bath
As we got older
We shared a laugh

You kicked a ball
I kicked it too
Everything I learnt
I learnt from you

Just three little kids
Fighting and crying
But best friends we became
Without even trying

Memories I cherish
With brothers I adore
Your little sister loves you
Right to her core

Shame

It's in your blood
It's under the sheets
It drenches your words
Like water in a flood

Shame on you
Shame on me
They'll always hate you
Because you shamed them too

With a carving knife
Straight to the chest
You pull it out
You end my life

You take your time
You make it hurt
You may have got hers
But you'll never have mine

Cracked Glass

It's crystal clear
With tiny cracks
But any depth
It sorely lacks

She sees right through
It's all right there
Behind a thin sheet
Covered with glare

She reaches out
It's cold to touch
It cuts her finger
It doesn't hurt much

That hard shiny exterior
That's all that you are
There's nothing left
But cracked glass and a scar

Knight in the Dark

I'm scared of the dark
Except when you're there
You light up my way
Glowing with love and care

Those horrible monsters
They don't scare me anymore
You slayed them and made me
Feel safe to my core

I can't even remember
Why I was so frightened
I turn over and you're there
And my heart is enlightened

I rebel against your help
Didn't want to be saved
But as it turns out
Your love is what my soul craved

You battle my demons
Carry me when I can't stand
You wear that suit of armour
And catch me before I can land

I've fallen into you
I know that much for sure
The moment our hearts touched
I knew fear no more

Stormflower

Can society tame
A woman born of fire
Or will they all be shamed
For calling her a liar

She will reign chaos
Down on all that doubt
She will bring the storm
With one last warning shout

They'll smash her to the pavement
Like dirt under their shoe
But she will only rise
Like she was always born to

A flower, a petal
Delicate she may seem
But she is truly a stormflower
A heart fighting to be seen

Haunted

By day you're a ghost
But by night I think I do
My dreams seem to tell me
That I'll always love you

You walked away
You broke what I gave
You turned it to dust
Buried in a shallow grave

You walk through my mind
Like a shadow in a corridor
Maybe you'll always own
A certain part of my core

I see you in it all
Everything I do
Because for me it was simple
It was always you

Lyla

She's oh so sassy
A soul so fierce
At two years old
My heart she will pierce

Gentle and strong
Curious and kind
She has a beautiful heart
That is so hard to find

This world can be cruel
Someday I'll tell you how
But it's so much brighter
Because you're in it now

Lyla you set a blaze
Like a bright burning flame
You came into this world
Our hearts you took claim

Pheonix Heart

With the heart of a Pheonix
And a sparkling diamond soul
That girl is on fire
Leaving a trail of coal

He breaks her to ashes
She explodes into flame
But she will only rise
Victory she'll claim

As strong as a diamond
As fierce as a fire
She will be reborn
A Pheonix heart that won't tire

A Flower and Her Grass

Like blades of grass
Around a flower
They'll fight to protect
With all their power

Edges so sharp
But beautiful to behold
They'll start out warm
And just as suddenly turn cold

Once you break the flower
The blades won't yield
They'll cut you down
Right in the field

You touch that petal
You make it bleed
But the grass will heal it
With a planted seed

Those beautiful best friends
Will fight to the death
To protect their flower
To their very last breath

www.ingramcontent.com/pod-product-compliance
Lightning Source LLC
LaVergne TN
LVHW021331200726

843509LV00014B/2490